At a
Fair

by **Dana Meachen Rau**

Reading Consultant: Nanci R. Vargus, Ed.D.

Marshall Cavendish
Benchmark
New York

Picture Words

 ball

 balloon

 clown

 cotton candy

 fair

 Ferris wheel

 fireworks

 hot dog

 merry-go-round

I like the .

I like the .

I like the .

I like to toss a .

I like a from a .

I like to eat a .

14

I like to eat .

16

I like to see .

The  is fun.

Words to Know

eat   (EET) to chew and swallow food

toss   to throw something lightly

Find Out More

Books

Burgess, Ron. *Be a Clown!: Techniques from a Real Clown*. Charlotte, VT: Williamson Publishing Company, 2001.

Cobb, Vicki. *Fireworks* (Where's the Science Here?). Brookfield, CT: Millbrook Press, 2005.

Videos

Dave Hood Entertainment. *Real Wheels: Here Comes a Roller Coaster*. Kid Vision.

Web Sites

National Confectioners Association: Cotton Candy History
http://www.candyusa.org/candy/cottoncandy.asp

The New England Carousel Museum
http://www.thecarouselmuseum.org/

About the Author

Dana Meachen Rau is an author, editor, and illustrator. A graduate of Trinity College in Hartford, Connecticut, she has written more than one hundred books for children, including nonfiction, biographies, early readers, and historical fiction. She likes to go to her local fair near Burlington, Connecticut, to watch the fireworks with her family.

About the Reading Consultant

Nanci R. Vargus, Ed.D., wants all children to enjoy reading. She used to teach first grade. Now she works at the University of Indianapolis. Nanci helps young people become teachers. She likes going to the state fair with her granddaughters, Corinne and Charlotte.

Marshall Cavendish Benchmark
99 White Plains Road
Tarrytown, NY 10591-9001
www.marshallcavendish.us

All Internet addresses were correct at the time of printing.

Library of Congress Cataloging-in-Publication Data

Rau, Dana Meachen, 1971–
At a fair / by Dana Meachen Rau.
     p. cm. — (Benchmark rebus)
Summary: Introduces the rides, snacks, and fun activities of a fair through simple text with rebuses.
Includes bibliographical references.
ISBN 978-0-7614-2606-6
1. Rebuses. [1. Fairs--Fiction. 2. Rebuses.] I. Title. II. Series.
PZ7.R193975Asr 2007
[E]--dc22
       2006031535

Editor: Christine Florie
Publisher: Michelle Bisson
Art Director: Anahid Hamparian
Series Designer: Virginia Pope

Photo research by Connie Gardner

Rebus images, with the exception of ball, cotton candy, fair, Ferris wheel and fireworks, provided courtesy of *Dorling Kindersley*.

Cover photo by Andreas Pollock/Taxi/Getty Images

The photographs in this book are used with the permission and through the courtesy of:
Superstock: p. 3 Ferris wheel, age footstock; p. 2 fair, Keith Kapple; *Corbis*: p. 3 ball, Jim Craigmoyle; p. 3 fireworks, Bill Ross; p. 2 cotton candy, James P. Blair; *Superstock*: p. 5, age footstock; p. 7, Gibson Stock Photography; *Image Works*: p. 9 Skjold Photographs; p. 19 Erin Moroney La Belle; *PhotoEdit*: p. 11 Tony Freeman; p. 13 Jeff Greenbert; *Alamy*: p. 17 Larry Brownstein; *Corbis*: p. 15 Barbara Peacock; p. 21 Tom and Dee Ann McCarthy.

Printed in Malaysia
1 3 5 6 4 2